Anger, because someone is driving slow in the left lane. Resentment because someone bullied me into a decision. Regret for not having the courage to speak up to someone. Sadness because there is no one patient enough to just sit and hear me out. Annoyed because right when I start to feel I'm doing well, there's a pit fall I stumble right into.

Life can throw at us curve balls, The world will continue to go with or without us, and people will carry their opinions or selfish ways regardless of how it is affecting us. We can see the attitude of another, the personality of another and we will gawk or mock then. We can see a situation all to which we can prescribe how it should have gone, or could have gone that would have been better off in the end. Or a way we know would have been, best.

All these situations and circumstances we think we can have an affect on and know a better way for, and are found in our every single day experiences. These are all situations that we believe we know something that is being unseen or not to 'their' knowledge. These are all situations that somehow, they are bringing us a stress, or a

situation to mock or gossip of.

When will I learn, this answer

is when I realize I just don't

know. I don't know the

situation, I don't know the

kind of day or morning they

have had or life they have

lived, I don't know if they are

struggling, I do not know if

someone will be open or closed

off. I do not know the best way,

a better way, or most

importantly I do not know their

way. Let a lone the idea, do I

even know my own way to

operate stress-free and

peaceful?

Continually bumping our

heads into similar situations,

stresses, or circumstances is
not by accident. It is a repeated
idea that we know something
so we act as though it is true,
when in fact it most likely is
not. We learn to adopt a
healthier, more affective way,
less of stress when we see that
we do not know. When we see
we know nearly, nothing. Let
go of that part of ourselves that

thinks we know, and accept

that we just don't know much.

Then, then we begin to learn.

Chapter 1
Freely curious

Coming to an internal standing ground where we accept we know nearly nothing, there we find an open field for exploration. We know nothing (much) means letting go of assumptions and expectations as well. We do not know the reason someone does

something, but that does not

mean we should assume it will

offend them if we ask. We do

not know why someone is

having a bad day, but that

does not mean they will be

rude if we ask. We do not know

what (that relative) that we

never really talk to (but

sometimes about) thinks of us,

we don't know their story,

experiences, or life. SO, ask.

There is no need to assume

anyone will ever think you are

odd, or ill informed, or dumb if

you ask. Most people… don't

know as well.

The beauty in learning that we

know nothing (much) is that

we open the doors wider to be

curious, to explore, and we see

that the more we experience,

take in and (learn) we see that

this is just, this one instance,

this is this experience, and

that even after 'learning' there

are still ways this same

encounter or thing will change,

grow, and be very different. We

come to a place that learning is

an enjoyable experience and "knowing" is actually less open minded, 'knowing' in many cases is a pidgon whole way of thinking, 'knowing' is well somewhat of a myth.

"When you're curious, you find lots of interesting things to do."

-Walt Disney

If someone 'knows' something, unless it is knowing that there is a God, that I know nothing (much), and I only have the ability to control my own feelings and response. Aside from these few things for someone to 'know' anything well just is nearly every time false. And yes I am going very literal with this idea. And that

is because why have any part
of ourself that is locked into
any one set idea that that is
the way it is, or must be. Why
say I know she is this way, I
know this will work, I know
what you mean, I know the
history of that ship. This or
that. To say I know, or I
already know is subconsouly
partially closing us off to any

other explanation. Let our minds be open to other possibilities, with is necessary a healthy cautiosness.

Changing 'I know' to; 'from my experience', 'to my knowledge', or 'the way I see it' doing this helps us keep the door open in our minds that there are other

ways to go about this, there
are other aspects I may have
not seen and from there we
can alter our view on this
topic, person, situation, or…
not. Doing this also allows for
others to see we are open
minded, we aren't closed off to
hearing their experience, and
we are showing we understand
there is more than one

perspective (millions) and there

is more than my own

experience with this subject,

topic or situation.

Keeping us in the state of

learning more so than the state

of being closed off as if we

'already know' keeps us in a

mindset that is more likely to

be freely curious.

Chapter 2
To learn what.. (?)

We are keeping an open mind to new experiences, or to learn new thing we may have overlooked, or to experience in a deeper or different way. To learn what exactly... nothing exactly. The idea that anything is ever completely fully learned though and though is very

unlikely. So what is the point
of this book? To learn to be
continually learning. To learn,
to continue to learn.

When will I learn, embodies the
idea that I have learned I cant
learn it all, that there is always
an aspect or angle of
everything and anything that is

yet to be discovered, and for

me to keep an open mind

makes for the best experience.

When will I learn brings us to

the idea that the ultimate

lesson is to continually learn of

to learn. How to learn new

ways, new flavors, new

relationships, emotions,

languages, people, places and

anything desired or
experienced.

To learn, the answer to when
will I learn, is when I learn to
appreciate learning over
knowing.

"I have no special talent. I am only passionately curious."

-Albert Einstein

Chapter 3
So now what?

Experience, go out and alter the perception of failure from a negative to an absolute positive. The word fail has gained a bit of a social stigma that I can not agree with, to me failing is learning. Failing is growth, failing is learning to have less and less fear and

more and more experience in
one given area.

Learning how we learn is a fun,
interesting and exciting road to
go down. Having a good
memory, good organizational
skills, good study habits, and
work ethic, imagine enhancing
these qualities by breaking

down our own innate nature to optimize ability in all areas we have passionate about in life.

Letting go of any idea that we know anything, and being open to continually search and or pioneer for a broader more expanded understanding. To keep in mind that there are still millions out there who 'know' this or that, we start to see how this looks, how

anything stuck in thinking

they know anything keeps

them, a fair bit stuck and

closed off.

Chapter 4
On the other end

To someone you're cute, to another your a snob, brat, tall, short, fat, mean, patient, helpful... most people take their perception as reality therefor, truth. Some People will believe their own thoughts about another without ever even meeting or talking with

that other person. We can
remember that they are
keeping themselves closed off
to you, and most likely many
others. If anyone has made
assumptions of you and thinks
they know you, this is not
uncommon to happen. That
does not mean we know
anything about this person
other than, they are most likely

struggling with their own

thoughts and ways of

operating.

"PEOPLE SUFFER BECAUSE THEY ARE CAUGHT IN THEIR VIEWS, AS SOON AS WE RELEASE THOSE VIEWS, WE ARE FREE AND WE DON'T SUFFER ANYMORE."

-Thick Nhat Hanh

There will always be someone
out there who thinks they
'know', weather they are
feeding their ego or feel inferior
and feel a need to prove they
'know' certain things, we can
simply remind ourselves of
how we used to operate within
thinking we 'knew'. And how
acknowledging we know nearly
nothing, and to open our own

doors to being curious to learn. How enjoyable and exciting life learning, new experiences and having an open mind is. How this person who claims to 'know' is most likely trapped, closing their own doors to openly learning and experiencing.

"*Be less curious about people, and more curious about ideas.*"

-Marie Curie

All the love and

encouragement,

-Britney Anne Klump

For more life learning

inspiration:

Instagram: @_Just.b___

Facebook: @just.b.llc

YouTube: Britney Anne

YouTube: Just.b The Island